FLOWERS

FLOWERS

An Illustrated Treasury

Compiled by Michelle Lovric

COURAGE BOOKS

an imprint of
RUNNING PRESS
Philadelphia, Pennsylvania

Canadian representatives: General Publishing Co., Ltd., 30 Lesmill Road, Don Mills, Ontario M3B 2T6.

9 8 7 6 5 4 3 2 1
Digit on the right indicates the number of this printing.

Library of Congress Cataloging-in-Publication
Number 92–50181
ISBN 1–56138–174–8
Text edited by Melissa Stein
Interior design by Stephanie Longo
Cover design by Toby Schmidt
Cover illustration by Vernon Ward
Typography by Commcor Communications Corporation, Philadelphia, Pennsylvania

Published by Courage Books, an imprint of
Running Press Book Publishers
125 South Twenty-second Street
Philadelphia, Pennsylvania 19103

The author gratefully acknowledges the permission of the following to reproduce copyrighted material in this book:

p. 11: From "The Garden" by Louise Glück, from *Descending Figure*, published by The Ecco Press. Copyright © Louise Glück 1976–80.

p. 19: From *A Year in the Country* by Alison Uttley, published by Faber & Faber Ltd., London, in 1957. Copyright © Alison Uttley 1976.

p. 30: From *Down the Garden Path* by Beverley Nichols, first published by Jonathan Cape, London, 1932, and reprinted in 1983 by The Antique Collector's Club, courtesy of Eric Glass Ltd. Copyright © Beverley Nichols 1983.

p. 22, 34: From *Green Thoughts: A Writer in the Garden*, by Eleanor Perényi, published by Random House Inc., New York and Allen Lane, London. Copyright © Eleanor Perényi 1981.

p. 42: From "Girl, Boy, Flower, Bicycle" by M. K. Joseph, courtesy of Mrs. M. J. Joseph.

p. 43: From *A Fairly Honorable Defeat* by Iris Murdoch, published by Chatto and Windus, London, and Viking Penguin, a division of Penguin Books U.S.A. Inc., New York. Copyright © Iris Alice Murdoch 1970.

INTRODUCTION

EVERYWHERE IN OUR LIVES, FLOWERS BLOOM. AS UNIVERSAL TOKENS OF LOVE, GRATITUDE, AND SYMPATHY, FLOWERS EMBRACE THE SENSES. A FLOWER DELIGHTS US WITH ITS BEAUTY AND FRAGRANCE, AND BECKONS OUR FINGERTIPS WITH ITS DELICATE PETALS.

IN THE LANGUAGE OF FLOWERS, LILIES SYMBOLIZE PURITY, AND LILACS, FIRST LOVE. MANY OTHER VARIETIES OF FLOWERS HAVE BEEN GATHERED BY WRITERS OF ALL ERAS AND CULTURES AS VIVID METAPHORS FOR DEVOTION, PASSION, AND THE TRANSIENCE OF LIFE.

TO ARTISTS, FLOWERS LEND THEIR GRACE AND COLOR. JUST AS WE ENJOY FLOWERS ALIVE, GROWING IN OUR GARDENS AND CAREFULLY TENDED GREENHOUSES, FLOWERS ALSO FLOURISH IN THE PAINTINGS ON OUR WALLS, ON THE GREETING CARDS THAT WE EXCHANGE, AND IN THE BOOKS THAT ENRICH OUR HOMES.

To

create

a little

flower

is the

labour

of ages.

WILLIAM BLAKE (1757–1827)
ENGLISH WRITER AND ARTIST

John Lancaster. 1971.

And we came to the Isle of
Flowers: their breath met us
out on the seas,
For the Spring and the middle
Summer sat each on the lap of
the breeze . . .
And the topmost spire of the
mountain was lilies in lieu of
snow,
And the lilies like glaciers winded
down, running out below
Thro' the fire of the tulip and
poppy, the blaze of gorse, and
the blush
Of millions of roses that sprang
without leaf or a thorn from
the bush . . .

ALFRED, LORD TENNYSON (1809–1892)
ENGLISH POET

The faint fresh flame of the young
year flushes
From leaf to flower and flower to
fruit.

ALGERNON SWINBURNE (1837–1909)
ENGLISH POET

EACH

FLOWER IS

A SOUL

BLOSSOMING

OUT TO

NATURE.

Gerard de Nerval [Gerard Labrunie] (1808–1855)
French writer

IT IS AT THE EDGE OF THE PETAL THAT LOVE WAITS.

William Carlos Williams (1883–1963)
American poet

Flowers are lovely; love is
flower-like.

SAMUEL TAYLOR COLERIDGE (1772–1834)
ENGLISH POET

The garden admires you.

For your sake it smears itself with green pigment,

the ecstatic reds of the roses,

so that you will come to it with your lovers.

LOUISE GLÜCK
20TH-CENTURY AMERICAN POET

eleven

And I will make thee beds
of roses
And a thousand fragrant
posies.

CHRISTOPHER MARLOWE (1565–1593)
ENGLISH DRAMATIST

thirteen

. . . WHAT GREATER DELIGHT IS

THERE THAN TO BEHOLD THE EARTH

APPARELLED WITH PLANTS, AS WITH A

ROBE OF EMBROIDERED WORK, SET

WITH ORIENT PEARLS AND GARNISHED

WITH GREAT DIVERSITY OF RARE AND

COSTLY JEWELS?

John Gerard (1545–1612)
English herbalist

I know a bank where the wild thyme blows,
Where oxlips and nodding violet grows,
Quite over-canopied with luscious woodbine,
With sweet musk-roses, and with eglantine.

WILLIAM SHAKESPEARE (1564–1616)
ENGLISH DRAMATIST

Everywhere the lanes were fragrant with Wild Roses, and Honeysuckle, and the breeze came to us over the hedges laden with the perfume of the clover-fields and grass-meadows...

EDITH HOLDEN (1871–1920)
ENGLISH NATURALIST

How graceful were those tiny plum blossoms,
The blurred vision of a lovely girl's face.
Furtive fragrance lingered with me as I went away;
I looked back and was pelted by hundreds of petals.

SU SHIH (1037–1101)
CHINESE POET

...the breath
of flowers is far
sweeter in the air
(where it comes and goes,
like the warbling of music)
than in the hand.

FRANCIS BACON (1561–1626)
ENGLISH PHILOSOPHER

I TRY TO DESCRIBE THEM BUT I HAVE NO WORDS FOR THOSE GOLDEN-BROWNS,

THOSE AMBER-GOLDS, THOSE TIGER-SCARLETS AND SHARP PINKS AND CITRON

YELLOWS AND CYCLAMEN ORANGES. THE LANGUAGE OF COLOR IS MUTED.

COLOR IS MUSIC, IT HAS THE RANGE OF MUSICAL NOTES, WITH SHARPS AND

CHORDS AND GLISSADES, AND ONLY MUSIC CAN PORTRAY THE COLOR OF

THESE FLOWERS.

Alison Uttley (1884–1976)
English writer

nineteen

twenty

A

morning-glory

at my window

satisfies me

more than the

metaphysics

of books.

WALT WHITMAN (1819–1892)
AMERICAN POET

Chide me not, laborious band!

For the idle flowers I brought;

Every aster in my hand

Goes home loaded with a

thought.

RALPH WALDO EMERSON (1803–1882)
AMERICAN WRITER

...I do believe that flowers have feelings, and that those feelings extend to the human beings who tend them.

ELEANOR PERÉNYI
20TH-CENTURY AMERICAN WRITER

I AM REALLY AS FOND OF MY GARDEN AS A YOUNG AUTHOR OF HIS FIRST PLAY.

Lady Mary Wortley Montagu (1690–1762)
English writer

Rare flower, leaf-fringed, of tender yellow gold—

Its sheen reflected on my studio window, penetrates the bamboo grove.

What could prevent a beautiful girl from casually smelling it?

I almost thought it was her lover's mouth imprinted in the center.

CHANG YU
NINTH-CENTURY CHINESE POET

*twenty·*FOUR

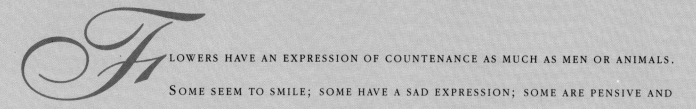

FLOWERS HAVE AN EXPRESSION OF COUNTENANCE AS MUCH AS MEN OR ANIMALS.

SOME SEEM TO SMILE; SOME HAVE A SAD EXPRESSION; SOME ARE PENSIVE AND

DIFFIDENT; OTHERS AGAIN ARE PLAIN, HONEST AND UPRIGHT, LIKE THE

BROAD-FACED SUNFLOWER AND THE HOLLYHOCK.

Henry Ward Beecher (1813–1887)
American cleric and writer

Gather

the flowers,

but spare

the buds.

ANDREW MARVELL (1621–1678)
ENGLISH POET

'Tis not I pity the flowers are about to die:

I only fear when flowers are gone age will hurry me on.

Lush branches too easily may be despoiled;

To these tender buds I say: you open a petal at a time.

TU FU (712-770)
CHINESE POET

FULL MANY A FLOWER IS BORN TO BLUSH UNSEEN, AND WASTE ITS SWEETNESS ON THE DESERT AIR. Thomas Gray (1716-1771) English poet

Any nose

May ravage with impunity a rose.

ROBERT BROWNING (1812–1889)
ENGLISH POET

These flowers which were splendid and sprightly, waking in the morning dawn's, will be a pitiful frivolity in the evening, falling asleep in the night's cold arms...

PEDRO CALDERON DE LA BARCA (1600–1681)
SPANISH WRITER

I have tried to catch [the] garden off its guard, without success. I always seem to arrive at the crowning hour of something or other. I have a feeling that as my car draws up at the door the stocks blaze into their ultimate, purple flames, the last of the lilies open their scented lips, the final rosebud sheds its virginity and flaunts itself in a southern breeze. Things are always at their very best when I visit... Perhaps if I stayed a little longer, till dusk fell, I might detect a weariness among the lilies, the stocks might droop, and on [the] hard pavements I might catch the echo of rose-leaves falling. But I never stay long...

BEVERLEY NICHOLS (1898–1983)
ENGLISH GARDENING WRITER

ow folds the lily all her sweetness up,

And slips into the bosom of the lake:

So fold thyself, my dearest, thou, and slip

Into my bosom and be lost in me.

Alfred, Lord Tennyson (1809–1892)
English poet

Time brings roses.

PORTUGUESE PROVERB

*W*hen

it comes

to roses,

some

of us

are

incurable.

Eleanor Perényi
20th-century American writer

And time remembered is grief forgotten,

And frosts are slain and flowers begotten,

And in green underwood and cover,

Blossom by blossom the spring begins.

ALGERNON SWINBURNE (1837–1909)
ENGLISH POET

You love the roses—so do I. I wish

The sky would rain down roses, as they rain

From off the shaken bush.

George Eliot [Mary Ann Evans] (1819–1880)
English novelist

There's rosemary, that's for remembrance;

pray, love, remember;

and there is pansies,

that's for thoughts.

WILLIAM SHAKESPEARE (1564–1616)
ENGLISH DRAMATIST

Lilies are white,
Rosemary's green,
When you are king,
I will be queen.

Roses are red,
Lavender's blue,
If you will have me,
I will have you.

ANONYMOUS

I HAVE HERE ONLY A NOSEGAY OF CULLED FLOWERS, AND HAVE BROUGHT

NOTHING OF MY OWN BUT THE THREAD THAT TIES THEM TOGETHER.

Michel Eyquem de Montaigne (1533–1592)
French essayist

ONE OF THE ATTRACTIVE THINGS ABOUT THE FLOWERS IS THEIR BEAUTIFUL RESERVE.

Henry David Thoreau (1817–1862)
American writer

To make a prairie it takes a clover
   and one bee,
One clover, and a bee,
And revery.
The revery alone will do,
If bees are few.

EMILY DICKINSON (1830–1886)
AMERICAN POET

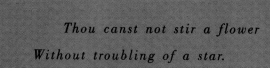

Thou canst not stir a flower
Without troubling of a star.

FRANCIS THOMPSON (1859–1907)
ENGLISH POET

Flowers

are the

sweetest

things

God

ever made

and forgot

to put

a soul into.

HENRY WARD BEECHER (1813–1887)
AMERICAN CLERIC AND WRITER

THE BUTTERCUP CATCHES THE SUN IN ITS CHALICE ....
James Russel Lowell (1819-1891) American poet

Simple and fresh and fair from winter's close emerging,

As if no artifice of fashion, business, politics, has ever been,

Forth from its sunny nook of shelter's grass—innocent, golden,

  calm as dawn,

The Spring's first dandelion shows its trustful face.

WALT WHITMAN (1819–1892)
AMERICAN POET

The girl . . . holds
a flower in her hand
A gold flower
In her hands she holds
The sun.

M. K. JOSEPH (1914–1981)
ENGLISH-BORN NEW ZEALAND WRITER

PEOPLE FROM A PLANET WITHOUT FLOWERS WOULD THINK WE MUST BE MAD WITH JOY THE WHOLE TIME TO HAVE SUCH THINGS ABOUT US.

Iris Murdoch, b. 1919
Irish-born English novelist

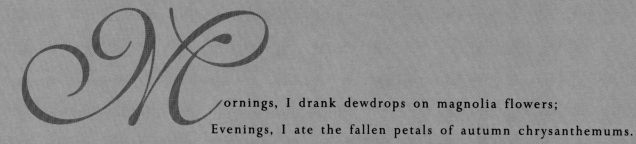

ornings, I drank dewdrops on magnolia flowers;
Evenings, I ate the fallen petals of autumn chrysanthemums.

CH'U YUAN (C. 343–278 B.C.)
CHINESE POET

Deep in their roots, all flowers keep the light.

THEODORE ROETHKE (1908–1963)
AMERICAN POET

ILLUSTRATION ACKNOWLEDGMENTS

COVER: *Primroses and Violets*, Vernon Ward

p.3: *Symphony in Blue and Pink*, Vernon Ward

p.7: *Spring*, John Lancaster

p.8, 9 [detail]: *Scarlet for the Garden*, Vernon Ward

p.10 [detail]: *Snowdrops*, Pamela Davis

p.11 [detail]: *Amatungula in Flower and Fruit and Blue Ipomoea, South Africa*, Marianne North (The Board of Trustees, Royal Botanic Gardens, Kew)

p.13: *A Basket of Roses*, Gerald Cooper

p.15: *Violet Time*, Vernon Ward

p.16: *Blue Carpet*, Vernon Ward

p.17 [detail]: *In the Conservatory*, James Tissot (Fine Art Photographic Library Limited)

p.18: *Spring Flowers*, John Strevens